INFOR
LONG

Why buy a guide book? Surely, everything you need to know is available online. True. But if you're like us, you don't want endless information, you want well-informed opinion. Less is more.

This book is an unapologetically short guide to the very best buildings to visit in London. It is a list according to us at Hoxton Mini Press, the informed minds of Sujata Burman and Rosa Bertoli and the brilliant eye of Taran Wilkhu. We aren't a slave to Brutalism or a servant of Modernism, we aren't worried about what is cool or if something is too touristic, but we do live in and love London and are fanatical about design and culture. These are the places we'd send you to if you came to visit us and wanted to go and see, touch and smell some astonishing buildings.

Ann and Martin
Founders, Hoxton Mini Press

Centre Point (no.10)

The Great Court, British Museum (no.14)

CONTRIBUTORS

Sujata Burman is a London-born and -based journalist, who has grown up with the architectural evolution of the city. She's currently Online Design Editor at *Wallpaper*,* bringing her design expertise to digital media. Her favourite London landmark? The 1930s Art Deco Hoover Building (no.47), for all its supermarket trolley-riding nostalgia.

Rosa Bertoli was born in Udine, Italy and now lives in London. As Design Editor of *Wallpaper*,* she's obsessed with the way different design, architecture and art merges and coexists. She's constantly discovering more of the city's diverse architectural landscape, from former power stations to Modernist and Brutalist gems.

Yorkshire-born *Taran Wilkhu* is a professional photographer who lives in south London in a timber-frame house designed by architect Walter Segal. Taran worked in travel, fashion, film and TV industries before turning his creativity and passion to photography. His lifestyle and architectural work has been featured in many publications such as *The Times*, *Guardian*, *The Telegraph*, *Dezeen* and *Monocle*.

FOREWORD

Buildings are stories. Literally. The word storey, a horizontal division of a building, is derived from *historia,* a medieval Latin word meaning a row of windows with pictures on them. There was a time, in fact, when it was pretty common to call any kind of pictorial or sculptural art containing figures – stained-glass windows, for example – a story.

Think then, what London must be – a vast library. Every building a book waiting to be read. Or rewritten. Retold. It's an appealing way to imagine what the city can be. And during the annual Open House Weekend in September each year, which gives free entry to London's best buildings and which my colleagues and I curate, we are always struck by the diversity of London's townscape and building stock and how their stories are not quite what you think at first.

Take James Stirling's No. 1 Poultry (no.6), a wonderful City of London block; an 80s design built in the 90s after its architect had passed away. And until what seems like just the other day, a building most critics regarded as a joke. Although now they're saying it's great – is that the joke? Or just another rewrite of its story, in a city forever remaking itself? Why do we change our minds about what's considered good? Or do buildings somehow improve, or worsen, depending on what sits alongside and around them? Or depending on our mood?

In the west, Peter Salter's Walmer Yard (no.42), another critic-divider – four interlocking houses, part Mackintosh, part Gaudí, part Carlo Scarpa. What kind of story does this gloomy sensorium tell, where the experience is one of touch, surface and deep, dark hues? Something both witty and absurd perhaps, some heavy entertainment. We don't have too many Gesamtkunstwerks – total works of art – in London, but Walmer Yard, the result of actually building a design by a renowned 'paper architect', is a special one.

Both of these unusual, challenging pieces of architecture, one moody, the other having a laugh, are listed in the book you're holding in your hands right now. It's a carefully thought-through edition – pretty much everything here is worthy of your time – and it cites buildings whose stories will leave you in a spin. At the Stirling Prize-winning Laban dance centre in Deptford (no.30), for example, by Tate Modern architects Herzog & de Meuron, check out the housing around that tries so hard to be in its gang. It's what happens when not-very-good architects (of which there are far too many, sadly) obsess about context – and get it wrong.

At Coal Drops Yard (no.49), there's a number of tales. Each shop unit for example, is scented. Is this evidence of a growing trend for London architects and citymakers to design with all the senses in mind? Or is the story here something else – like what happens when British architecture's twin obsessions – the icon (yes, still) and heritage (of course heritage!) – literally wrap around each other in this biggest yet of Thomas Heatherwick's London buildings?

How about the Walkie Talkie (no.17), its bulging façade, clearly inspired by a banker's waistline after a boozy conspiratorial lunch? In this respect it's perfect, surely. Try not to hate it. (And don't be too surprised if you find you quite like it.)

Nothing in London is what it seems at first glance. Or maybe our best buildings are many-faceted things. Like Patrick Hodgkinson's Brunswick Centre (no.3), famed for its massive... Waitrose? And its soaring Sant'Elia-inspired elevations too, of course, thrusting upwards into the skies and longwards, facing off against Bloomsbury's yellow-brown brick façades...

You'll get lost in this book. It's full of stories, none of them short.

Rory Olcayto
Director, Open House London

Open House London is a weekend festival held in September each year which offers free public access to hundreds of buildings, many usually private or charging an entry fee. 'Open House' is mentioned alongside entries in this book when a building is not open to the public otherwise. Please note the selection changes annually. For more information, please visit www.openhouselondon.org.uk.

GLOSSARY

*Explaining a few of the dominant styles shaping
London's architectural landscape*

Neoclassical. Taking cues from the Greeks and the Romans, these structures scream grandeur and old-school opulence. Throughout London, this revivalist style often merges with Contemporary structures – case in point, the British Museum's dramatic Great Court (no.14).

Victorian. Named after the era's reigning monarch, this genre saw architects experimenting with symmetry, drawing from other types of architecture such as Gothic Revival and Classical, and using materials like iron and slate. See Smithfield Market (no.12) and Kew Gardens (no.48).

Industrial. Factories built during and after the industrial revolution – power stations and coal yards included – are today's pivotal, and functional, landmarks. A style rarely seen outside the UK: think Tate Modern (no.25) and Battersea Power Station (no.32).

Modernism. In the post-war era, London looked at how European cities were innovating urban landscapes to cleverly rebuild the city with this form-follows-function approach. Structures are minimalist, compact and a touch nostalgic; see Isokon Flats (no.52) and Royal College of Physicians (no.50).

Art Deco vs Art Nouveau. Born in the late 19th century, Nouveau is inspired by artistry and expression: see the Whitechapel Gallery (no.19). Its younger sister Deco followed in the 1920s with signatures including experimental use of colour and pattern, ie. Michelin House (no.43); and elegant detailing, eg. Eltham Palace (no.29).

Brutalism. It's a love/hate subcategory of Modernism, mainly formed during the 1970s when raw concrete was given new use in pioneering monolithic structures. Now they are listed masterpieces, such as the Barbican (no.8), Centre Point (no.10) and The National Theatre (no.33)

Postmodernism. PoMo is the bold, irreverent counter-argument to the subdued, clean and functional lines of Modernism. Check out candy-striped No. 1 Poultry (no.6) and colourful 1980s Isle of Dogs Pumping Station (no.23).

Deconstructivism. This division of PoMo focuses on more rebellious shapes that reject both geometry and symmetry. Saw Swee Hock Centre's asymmetric brick puzzle (no.1) and Zaha Hadid's wave-like Aquatics Centre (no.18) are some of our finest examples.

Contemporary. All of the above styles play a part in inspiring this 21st-century aesthetic – from high-tech structures like The Shard (no.31), to experimental innovation, such as the sustainable Bloomberg HQ (no.7) and multi-sensory Sun Rain Rooms (no.13). There's much more to come, so watch this space...

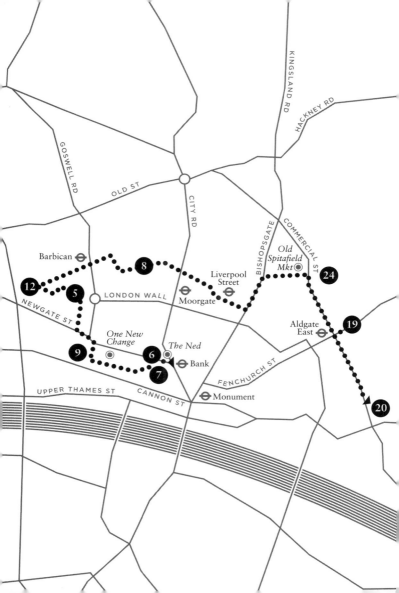

WALK 1

*A historical throwback around
the city's heritage treasures*

Begin with breakfast at The Ned*, inside the vast former
1920s Midland Bank, before taking in the PoMo façade of
6 No. 1 Poultry. Around the corner is **7** Bloomberg HQ
(free entry to the arcade), a shining example of sustainable
design; don't miss the reconstruction of the Roman road
and third-century Temple of Mithras originally discovered
here. Continue with a tour of one of London's oldest landmarks, **9** St Paul's (paid entry), then go for a rooftop drink
at Jean Nouvel's One New Change*, for a view of the
cathedral's Portland stone dome.

Head east to **5** Maggie's Barts (grounds open to the
public), before walking via the 19th-century **12** Smithfield
Market towards **8** Barbican's Brutalist universe (open to
the public). Next, take a 20-minute stroll over to **24** Fournier
Street for a taste of Georgian London, then grab some food
at Old Spitalfields Market* nearby. Get a culture fix with the
latest art exhibition at **19** Whitechapel Gallery (paid entry);
and a sundowner and a show at **20** Wilton's Music Hall
(paid entry), which still holds the magic of the old Victorian
East End.

*Walking time: 1-1.5 hours, 3.8 miles
Total time with stops: 3-6 hours
Not in guide book; more info online

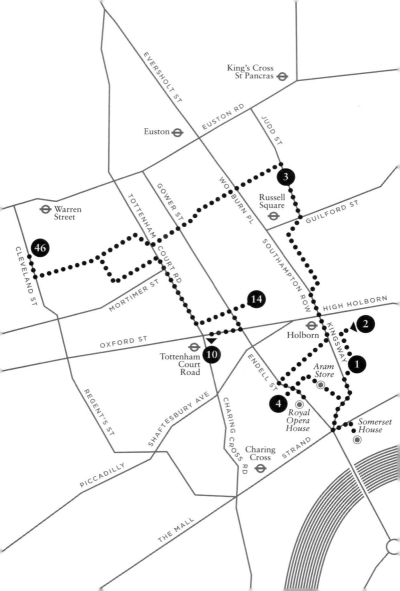

WALK 2

*A short tour of Contemporary style
and brilliant Brutalism*

Begin at ② Sir John Soane's treasure trove of three magnificent Georgian houses that make up the museum (free entry), then wander over to the ① Saw Swee Hock Centre to admire its puzzle-like façade (open to the public). If it's near lunchtime, we recommend Spring's seasonal menu at nearby Somerset House* – allow time for an exhibition here too – then move on to browse modern design emporium Aram*.

Over the road in Covent Garden's Floral Street, walk under the dancing silhouette of the ④ Bridge of Aspiration, before stopping for coffee at the Royal Opera House's café*, designed by Stanton Williams. Hit the ③ Brunswick Centre (open to the public) next for a Brutalism fix, then immerse yourself in ㊻ RIBA's peaceful bookshop. The all-encompassing ⑭ Great Court at the British Museum is a good place to sit back and take a moment (free entry).

Finally, wander into town or stop for early dinner and/or 1960s cocktails at VIVI restaurant inside concrete icon ❿ Centre Point.

Walking time: 1.5-2 hours, 4.8 miles
Total time with stops: 3-6 hours
*Not in guide book; more info online

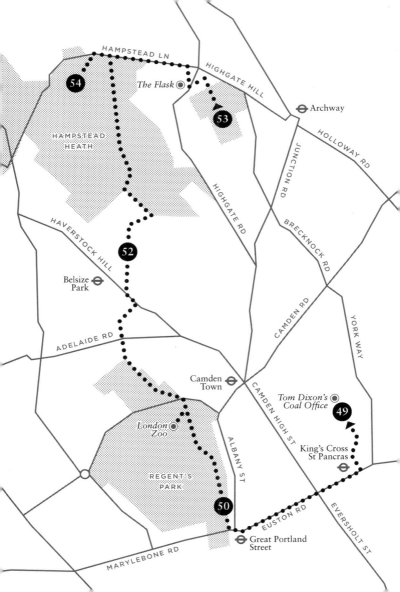

WALK 3

*A journey from Neoclassicism to Modernism
via London's best park life*

Start your day with a tour of **53** Highgate Cemetery (paid entry) and its to-die-for stonework before dissecting the tales of its eclectic occupants over a pint, or lunch, at The Flask pub*. Shake off any lingering spooks with a brisk walk over to the Neoclassical **54** Kenwood House (free entry) and its sun-trap landscaped gardens. Continue through one of London's finest green spaces, Hampstead Heath, and arrive at Modernist haven **52** Isokon Flats (free access to the gallery), former home to spies, creatives and Agatha Christie herself.

Walk via Primrose Hill to London Zoo to discover another concrete masterpiece: the Grade I listed Penguin Pool by Berthold Lubetkin* (paid entry to Zoo). Walk on to the **50** Royal College of Physicians (free entry) – don't miss its medicinal gardens.

Finish by exploring the redeveloped King's Cross area; spot subtle hints of its Victorian past in Thomas Heatherwick's **49** Coal Drops Yard (free entry), browse the many shops and eateries here, or for something special head to Tom Dixon's Coal Office restaurant*.

Walking time: 2-3 hours, 7.6 miles
Total time with stops: 4-6 hours
*Not in guide book; more info online

1

LSE SAW SWEE HOCK CENTRE

A Deconstructivist jigsaw brick marvel

At the centre of the village-like campus of the London School of Economics lie the angular forms of the Saw Swee Hock Centre. Built using 17,000 locally sourced, hand-made bricks, architects O'Donnell & Tuomey have referred to the highly sustainable structure as their 'Japanese puzzle'. Inside, a sweeping concrete staircase, terrazzo details and red accents provide the missing pieces; while all the student essentials, from a career centre to a pub, make it a fresher's favourite. Stroll through the pedestrian lanes and take in different perspectives of the asymmetric, dynamic façade.

Nearest station: Holborn
Address: 1 Sheffield Street, WC2A 2AP
Architect: O'Donnell & Tuomey Architects (2015)
Access: Free entry
Visitor info: sawsweehockcentre.com

2

SIR JOHN SOANE'S MUSEUM

A Georgian masterpiece crammed with relics

A treasure trove of Sir John Soane's collectables lies in these three townhouses. The domestic spaces are packed with the architect's paintings and historic artefacts, one of the most extraordinary pieces being the alabaster sarcophagus of Pharaoh Seti, direct from Ancient Egypt. Everything is exactly as it was when Soane lived here, thanks to his negotiations with Parliament to keep it that way after his death and ensure it remained a free public gallery. Wander through the spectacular labyrinth of rooms, under the canopy ceilings, and let the stories unfold around you.

Nearest station: Holborn
Address: 13 Lincoln's Inn Fields, WC2A 3BP
Architect: Sir John Soane (1813)
Access: Free entry
Visitor info: soane.org

3

THE BRUNSWICK CENTRE

A Brutalist shopping complex

Back in the 1970s, this megastructure was handed over from architect Patrick Hodgkinson to Camden council, and, in his words, turned into a 'council housing ghetto'. But, in the late 1990s he was given an opportunity to resurrect his vision for a clever cluster of mixed-use social housing. He enlisted Levitt & Bernstein for the job and now the white concrete superblock is part shopping centre, part residential, and on a sunny day, the bold, stepped design resembles a Mediterranean holiday complex. Bypass Waitrose and the usual chain restaurants and instead wander through to the Curzon cinema and second-hand bookshop, Skoob, tucked away in the basement.

Nearest station: Russell Square
Address: Bernard Street, WC1N 1BS
Architects: Patrick Hodgkinson (1972),
David Levitt & David Bernstein (2006)
Access: Shopping centre open to the public
Visitor info: brunswick.co.uk

4

ROYAL BALLET SCHOOL'S BRIDGE OF ASPIRATION

A Contemporary twisting, dancing bridge

It's easy to miss this clever concertina of a sky bridge as you navigate the ever-packed Covent Garden. So, take this as a heads up. A connector between the Royal Opera House and the Royal Ballet School, the bridge consists of 23 square portals that make an elegant quarter-turn around their aluminium frame, designed to reflect the movements of dancers inside. Forget the view from the bridge though, it's all about catching it at golden hour from street level, for a shimmering recital of metal and glass.

Nearest station: Covent Garden
Address: 44 Floral Street, WC2E 9DG
Architect: Wilkinson Eyre (2003)
Access: View from street (no public access)

5

MAGGIE'S BARTS
Architecture for hope

This cancer support centre reminds us that great architecture can uplift and bring hope to those in need. Architect Steven Holl fulfilled the vision of Maggie Keswick Jencks and her husband, architectural historian Charles Jencks, with a layered composition of bamboo, concrete and translucent matte glass, seamlessly attached to the 12th-century St Bartholomew's Hospital in Smithfield. Vibrant geometric symbols, relating to both the medieval and Greek notions of 'life force', are woven into the very fabric of the building. A truly inspirational place.

Nearest station: Barbican
Address: St Bartholomew's Hospital, ECIA 7BE
Architect: Steven Holl Architects (2017)
Access: St Bartholomew's grounds open to the public

6

NO. 1 POULTRY

Postmodernist giant in the heart of the city

While this site was originally intended for a tower by
Mies van der Rohe, purist fans have since been swayed
by James Stirling's Postmodernist colossus, which
pipped van der Rohe to the post. The soaring stripy
limestone façade, clock face, and busy composition
of columns and glass bring playful energy to an otherwise hectic junction. Inside, beyond the atrium of blue
glazed tiles and colourful window frames, is a branch
of WeWork's office space – and hotel and members'
joint The Ned, Jean Nouvel's retail destination
One New Change and the Bloomberg HQ (no.7)
are all neighbours.

Nearest station: Bank
Address: 1 Poultry, EC2R 8EJ
Architect: James Stirling (1997)
Access: Rooftop restaurant open to the public

7

BLOOMBERG HQ

Office of the future with a taste of the past

This Stirling Prize-winner was recognised as the most sustainable office building in the world in 2017. It scores eco points via bronze fins, angled to create shade and ventilation, a petal-shaped aluminium ceiling for efficient cooling, an on-site treatment plant to reuse rainwater and a green living wall. Plus, environmentally inspired artworks, including Olafur Eliasson's rippling metallic sculpture and Cristina Iglesias' water-and-bronze installation. Although made for the future, it's a true ode to the past – head below ground, where they have reinstated part of the ancient Roman road and the third-century Temple of Mithras that originally stood here.

Nearest station: Bank
Address: 3 Queen Victoria Street, EC4N 4TQ
Architect: Foster & Partners (2017)
Access: Restaurants on ground floor open to the public;
free entry to Mithraeum, pre-booking advised
Visitor info: bloombergarcade.com

8

THE BARBICAN ESTATE

London's finest example of Brutalism

What makes the Barbican a London icon? Well, there's nothing quite like this mini metropolis of groundbreaking post-war Brutalism, which took over a decade to build. It's tough on the outside, with a calming cultural hub beneath the surface. Explore the monolithic space via waterways, fountains, gardens and most futuristically, elevated pedways – routes that escape the traffic below. Head inside for the theatre, gallery, restaurants and bars; or go on a pre-planned Sunday for the joy of the Conservatory and its forest of tropical plants and trees that wrap around the concrete silhouette, softening the edges a little.

Nearest station: Barbican
Address: Silk Street, EC2Y 8DS
Architect: Chamberlin, Powell & Bon (1976/1982)
Access: Free entry to many areas; Conservatory open on
selected Sundays, see website; paid entry to exhibitions
Visitor info: barbican.org.uk

9

ST PAUL'S CATHEDRAL

London's English Baroque centrepiece

Out of all of London's landmarks, St Paul's has the ultimate staying power. When its original structure was ravaged by The Great Fire in 1666, Sir Christopher Wren got straight to the mammoth task of rebuilding, and the authoritative Portland stone dome was completed in 1708. Since then, it has withstood the Blitz and remains a cosmic icon on the skyline today. Inside, baroque features are all-encompassing, from the crypt to the grand nave, and there's an overriding sense of being right at the city's historic heart. Explore the cathedral's anatomy via a guided tour, and gain a little perspective from the surrounding gardens.

Nearest station: St Paul's
Address: St Paul's Churchyard, EC4M 8AD
Architect: Sir Christopher Wren (1711)
Access: Paid entry
Visitor info: stpauls.co.uk

10

CENTRE POINT

An intricate Brutalist icon

Like many of London's reinforced concrete beasts, Centre Point hasn't always been popular. Situated at the dodgier end of Oxford Street, this 1960s tower – one of the first skyscrapers in London – fell into decline at the end of the 20th century. Cue a recent revival, which ushered in luxury penthouses, restaurants and retail. Get up close to appreciate its Grade II listed, graphic façade; the level of intricacy creates the effect of a drawing made from stone. It's a happier story than that of its Brutalist neighbour, Welbeck Street car park, which is set for demolition.

Nearest station: Tottenham Court Road
Address: 103 New Oxford Street, WC1A 1DB
Architects: Richard Seifert & Partners (1966),
Conran & Partners (2018)
Access: Restaurant open to the public

11

LLOYD'S BUILDING

The high-tech home of global insurance

The guts of this building – including lifts, bathrooms, pipework and mechanics – live on the outside; a clever move by the architects, allowing insurance broker Lloyd's of London to monopolise the inside. Rogers et al pioneered a trading floor that expands via a series of galleries; while the steel-clad frame gives Gothic attitude, towering above people traffic, like high-tech artwork against the 19th-century Leadenhall Market. In 2011, it joined the select club of Modernist Grade I listed structures – just what every building wants for its 25th birthday. Tip: sweet talk the Lloyd's CEO for an invite to dine in the private, 1763 reconstructed Adam Room.

Nearest station: Bank
Address: 1 Lime Street, EC3M 7AW
Architect: Richard Rogers & Partners (1986)
Access: View from street (no public access)

12

SMITHFIELD MARKET

London's Victorian meat market

Dating from the 10th century, Smithfield is the largest wholesale meat market in the UK and, aside from animals, has also seen a few executions over the centuries. The Grade II listed building by Sir Horace Jones still features the original cast iron, stone, Welsh slate and glass, and remains a grand setting for butchers to trade within. There are rumours the meat market may move out of the capital though, so while you still can, experience the full buzz between 2am and 7am; and if you're local, don't miss the drama of Christmas Eve's meat auction.

Nearest station: Farringdon
Address: Grand Avenue, EC1A 9PS
Architect: Sir Horace Jones (1868)
Access: Free entry (2-7am),
closed on weekends and bank holidays
Visitor info: smithfieldmarket.com

13

SUN RAIN ROOMS
Elemental house expansion

This isn't just any Portland stone Georgian townhouse, it's a front for something far more exciting. Behind the façade lies a multi-seasonal extension: a steel pipe outlining the plywood roof collects rainfall and filters it down in a calming rain dance. This whirlpool installation mirrors the architecture, while in summer, the sweeping roof becomes a sky garden, featuring Himalayan cedar and Japanese umbrella pine. The innovative space is now used as a studio for Tonkin Liu architects, but visit during Open House (please check the website as it's not included every year), and, rain or shine, you are in for a treat.

Nearest station: Angel
Address: 5 Wilmington Square, WC1X 0ES
Architect: Tonkin Liu (2017)
Access: Free entry during Open House
(check website as it may not be included every year)
Visitor info: openhouselondon.org.uk

14

BRITISH MUSEUM

A Classical monolith of calm

At the heart of this cultural institution is the Great Court – the largest, and arguably most extraordinary, covered courtyard in Europe. Added in 2000, consider this proof that the architecture of one era really can be enhanced by another. And if the promise of a vast two-acre, two-century-old Greek Revivalist masterpiece isn't enough, it's topped by a hypnotic tessellated glass roof. Architecture turns artwork with geometric shadow patterns cast across the light-filled space. Explore the museum's renowned archive of artefacts; or just sit back in what is one of central London's most serene meeting spots.

Nearest station: Holborn
Address: Great Russell Street, WC1B 3DG
Architects: Sir Robert Smirke (1852), Foster & Partners (2000)
Access: Free entry
Visitor info: britishmuseum.org

15

MILLENNIUM BRIDGE

River Thames' floating sculpture

Walking over Millennium Bridge is always magical, thanks to the merging of brilliant architectural minds, Foster & Partners, with sculptor Anthony Caro and engineers Arup. It's currently the only pedestrian bridge over the Thames, and with the Tate Modern (no.25) on the South Bank, and St Paul's (no.9) and the City on the north, the views give a real sense of being in the company of London's finest. Its nicknames range from 'the wobbly bridge' due to a less than stable start (don't worry, it's secure now), to 'the blade of light' – head over at sunset or sunrise for the full effect.

Nearest station: Mansion House
Address: Thames Embankment, SE1 9JE
Architect: Foster & Partners (2000)
Access: Open to the public

16

M BY MONTCALM

Op Art hotel in the city's tech hub

As its nickname – 'Optical Illusion' – suggests, this building is made for visual trickery. Inspired by its neighbour, Moorfields Eye Hospital, and Op Art maestro Bridget Riley, the architects have designed the pointed structure in reverse perspective, which can make it look radically different at various times of the day due to the light, shadows and reflections. Its concerto of lines and diagonal shapes is a powerful addition to the busy Shoreditch skyline – just don't look directly at it for too long or it'll make you dizzy.

Nearest station: Old Street
Address: 151-157 City Road, EC1V 1JH
Architects: Squire & Partners, Executive Architects 5 Plus (2015)
Access: Restaurant open to the public;
hotel rooms available to book
Visitor info: mbymontcalm.co.uk

17

20 FENCHURCH STREET

A sky-high garden refuge

Red hot poker, bird of paradise, French lavender and rosemary are just a few of the botanicals freshening up the landscaped Sky Garden, on floors 35 to 37 of the 'Walkie Talkie' (so called for its top-heavy, curved shape). During its construction in 2013, it hit a hurdle when the heat of its solar reflection caused nearby cars to melt – literal deconstructive architecture. Once completed though, London's unofficial highest park won us all over: the oasis includes restaurants, bars and, of course, an obligatory outdoor viewing platform.

Nearest station: Monument
Address: 20 Fenchurch Street, EC3M 4BA
Architect: Rafael Viñoly (2014)
Access: Restaurants and bars open to the public;
free entry to viewing platform, pre-booking essential
Visitor info: skygarden.london

18

LONDON AQUATICS CENTRE

Zaha Hadid's futuristic swimming arena

Dive in to the 50-metre pools here to fully experience what Zaha Hadid was aiming for – an expansive space where swimmers would feel a sense of total immersion. Created for the 2012 Olympics and opened to the public in 2014, the Aquatics Centre is flooded with natural light thanks to windows that span its length, complemented by wood, steel and concrete interiors. The wave-inspired silhouette has strong competition across the park: the Stadium by Populous; Velodrome by Hopkins Architects; and Anish Kapoor and Cecil Balmond's ArcelorMittal Orbit tower (for cheap thrills, slide down the world's tallest and longest tunnel slide, by Carsten Höller).

Nearest station: Stratford
Address: Queen Elizabeth Olympic Park, E20 2ZQ
Architect: Zaha Hadid Architects (2011)
Access: Paid entry, no pre-booking required
Visitor info: londonaquaticscentre.org

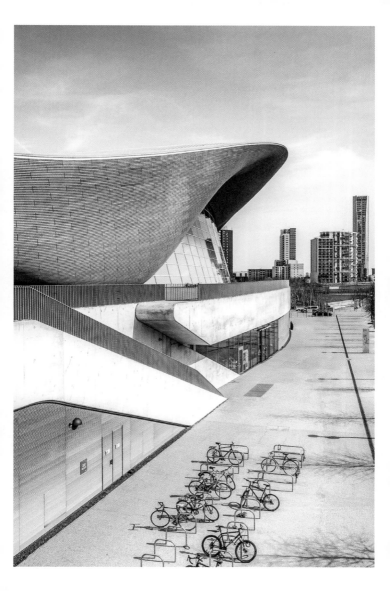

19

WHITECHAPEL GALLERY

East London's contemporary art destination

Transforming an area known in the 1900s for crime, this Art Nouveau gallery opened in 1901 with the aim of 'bringing great art to the people of East London'. And it remains true to that mission statement today. The discreetly striking façade showcases artist Rachel Whiteread's *Tree of Life*: foliage cast in bronze and plated in gold, to mirror the urban plants wrapped around surrounding buildings. Inside, it has hosted works by the likes of Donald Judd, Mark Rothko, Frida Kahlo, and, in 1939, the only UK showing of Picasso's *Guernica*. The Refectory, by the duo behind Soho's 10 Greek Street, is a bonus culinary treat.

Nearest station: Aldgate East
Address: 77-82 Whitechapel High Street, E1 7QX
Architects: Charles Harrison Townsend (1901), Robbrecht en Daem and Witherford Watson Mann Architects (2009)
Access: Free entry to some galleries; paid entry to exhibitions
Visitor info: whitechapelgallery.org

20

WILTON'S MUSIC HALL
Victorian theatre set

Hidden down a Whitechapel backstreet, this site has been cleverly restored to ensure its street lanterns, exposed brickwork and historic staircases transport you right back to the Victorian bolthole it once was. Originally built as five houses, it became an alehouse and concert hall, then a Methodist's Mission in response to extreme poverty in the late 1800s. Various musicians filmed videos here in its derelict days (including Annie Lennox and Frankie Goes To Hollywood), drawn to the undeniable atmosphere. Today, come for a pint and a performance in the barrel-vaulted auditorium, surrounded by memorabilia offering salacious tales from ye olde East End.

Nearest station: Aldgate East
Address: 1 Graces Alley, E1 8JB
Architects: John Wilton (1859), Tim Ronalds (2015)
Access: Free entry to bar; paid entry to shows,
pre-booking advised
Visitor info: wiltons.org.uk

21

ST PAUL'S BOW COMMON

A Modernist-Brutalist place of worship

Far from your usual Gothic religious architecture, this post-war church digresses down a much more Modernist, almost Brutalist, route. All but destroyed by WWII bombing, the original building was demolished to make way for the new, completed in 1960. Its geometric glass roof and purple brick façade are award-winning, while equally bold interiors feature Murano mosaics by artist Charles Lutyens and a cascade of natural light illuminating the concrete. The missive, 'This is the gate of heaven', carved over the entrance by German sculptor Ralph Beyer, has been adopted by the local parish as the church's unofficial name.

Nearest station: Mile End
Address: St Paul's Way, E3 4AR
Architect: Robert Maguire & Keith Murray (1960)
Access: Open to the public
Visitor info: stpaulsbowcommon.org.uk

22

RIO CINEMA

Cult Art Deco movie house

Of all the Art Deco cinemas in the city, this is the leader for retro nostalgia. It comes alive after dark, a romantically lit beacon drawing crowds to its corner of Kingsland High Street. Once an auctioneer's shop, it's one of London's first picture houses, established by businesswoman Clara Ludski in 1915. Today's auditorium was created in 1937 in the shell of the original space; and through a trapdoor in the roof, echoes of the old cinema can still be seen. Book in for a cult classic throwback (or a new release), and have a pre-movie drink in the basement bar.

Nearest station: Dalston Kingsland
Address: 107 Kingsland High Street, E8 2PB
Architects: George Coles (1915), FE Bromige (1937)
Access: Paid entry to film screenings
Visitor info: riocinema.org.uk

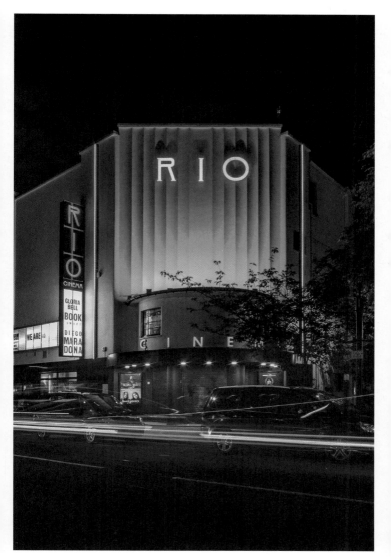

23

ISLE OF DOGS PUMPING STATION

Postmodernist pumphouse

If you've walked all the way along the Thames to the Isle of Dogs, you're probably lost. But, before you backtrack, get a picture of this colourful 1980s riverside curiosity, dubbed 'Temple of Storms'. It's still in use today, pumping excess water directly into the river during stormy weather to prevent flooding; and while you can't go inside, the exterior is what takes it from purely functional to unforgettable. Elevated to Grade II listed status in 2017, it's perhaps one of the most unexpected and exciting examples of rebellious Postmodernist architecture in London.

Nearest station: Canary Wharf
Address: Stewart Street, E14 3YH
Architect: John Outram (1988)
Access: View from street (no public access)

24

FOURNIER STREET

An architectural slice of East End history

For a real taste of Georgian London, take a walk down this street. Running from Spitalfields' Christ Church to Brick Lane, its 18th-century houses are spectacularly preserved. The area is a testament to the cultural groups who have lived here, from the original French silk-weaving Huguenots to Jewish and Bengali communities, as well as art students and artists – Gilbert and George and Tracey Emin among them. The brick façades, large windows and soberly painted shutters offer respite from the modern hipster mood, epitomised by the 1740s sundial with its Latin inscription 'Umbra Sumus' – we are shadows.

Nearest station: Liverpool Street
Address: Fournier Street, E1
Architects: Various (18th century)
Access: Street accessible to the public

25

TATE MODERN

The ultimate Industrial art museum

Yes, South Bank can be a tourist trap. But, for the Tate Modern, it's worth making an exception. Converted from the disused Bankside Power Station in the late 1990s, there's a reason it's now one of the world's top geo-tagged museums on Instagram. Modern art and Industrial architecture combine to create a truly dynamic space: from the vast Turbine Hall – which artists, including Ai Weiwei and Louise Bourgeois, have used to frame immersive works – to the dramatic concrete staircase in the latest extension, Switch House. Discover live art in the former oil tanks, then head up to the 10th floor viewing platform for that Instagram-worthy panoramic.

Nearest station: Southwark
Address: Bankside, SE1 9TG
Architects: Giles Gilbert Scott (1963),
Herzog & de Meuron (2000/2016)
Access: Free entry; paid entry to temporary exhibitions
Visitor info: tate.org.uk

26

OXO TOWER WHARF

Art Deco jewel on the South Bank

This riverside Art Deco monument offers some of the city's finest power station architecture (it once sourced electricity exclusively to the Royal Mail Post Office). The eponymous stock cube producers took over in the 1920s, and to get around the law that forbid skyline advertising on South Bank, they commissioned a series of decorative windows that incorporated their iconic lettering – the rebels. Perhaps the best money they've spent on marketing too, as the brick tower remains intact. Inside, beyond the colonnade, the meaty essence has been replaced by a hub of studios, shops, galleries and restaurants.

Nearest station: Blackfriars
Address: Barge House St, SE1 9PH
Architects: Albert Moore (1929),
Lifschutz Davidson Sandilands (1996)
Access: Restaurants, shops and galleries open
to the public; no access to tower (seen overleaf)
Visitor info: oxotower.co.uk

27

RIVOLI BALLROOM

Hidden theatre of Art Deco glamour

Dress up in your finest, grab a partner and swing your way back to the 1950s at Rivoli Ballroom. Still as exuberantly Art Deco as it was back then, the barrel-vaulted auditorium is the only dance hall of its kind left in London, a transformation of an early 20th-century cinema. Inside, it's unexpectedly vast, doing its best to upstage you with plush red velvet walls framed with gold gilt, oriental lanterns, dark boudoirs and train carriage-style booths. From jive nights to cabaret and film screenings – it's kitsch, fabulous and the place to live out your secret ballroom dancing dreams.

Nearest station: Brockley
Address: 350 Brockley Road, SE4 2BY
Architect: Henley Attwater (1913)
Access: Ticketed events, pre-booking essential
Visitor info: rivoliballroom.com

28

DULWICH PICTURE GALLERY

World's first purpose-built public art space

When Sir Peter Francis Bourgeois left his collection to Dulwich College in 1811, he asked his friend Sir John Soane to create something unheard of: a public art gallery. Soane delivered a seemingly endless space, framed by interior arches, painted picture-gallery red, with roof lanterns that cast a dreamy natural light. Today, a glass corridor connects his Classical structure with new expansions. Bourgeois's spirit lives on, too: he's buried in the mausoleum. As soon as the sun's out (wishful thinking), visit the pop-up pavilion, designed by different creative talents every other year.

Nearest station: West Dulwich
Address: Gallery Road, SE21 7AD
Architects: Sir John Soane (1817), Rick Mather (2000)
Access: Paid entry
Visitor info: dulwichpicturegallery.org.uk

29

ELTHAM PALACE

Lavish Art Deco mansion

The architectural evolution of this manor was influenced by its occupants: from Henry VIII to the British Army, it changed drastically with each owner. The original medieval palace was war-torn in the 1600s and left unloved for centuries – at one point, the magnificent great hall was downgraded to a farmhouse barn. Fast forward to the 20th century and enter the Courtaulds, millionaires and global nomads who transformed it into a glorious Art Deco home in the 1930s. Enlisting young architects Seely & Paget, they prioritised luxury, from ornate marquetry walls in the domed entrance hall to a glossy gold tile and marble bathroom.

Nearest station: Mottingham
Address: Court Yard, SE9 5QE
Architects: Rolf Engströmer (14th century),
Seely & Paget (1933)
Access: Paid entry
Visitor info: english-heritage.org.uk/elthampalace

30

LABAN BUILDING

Lyrical composition of colour

There is a poetic choreography in the architectural DNA of this building, home to the Trinity Laban Conservatoire of Music and Dance. Outside – against the urban backdrop of Deptford Creek – iridescent stained glass panels, developed by artist Michael Craig-Martin, cover the bold block structure. Inside, you're met by Herzog & de Meuron's trademark centre stage: a monolithic staircase, leading up to the main theatre. The multi-disciplinary space includes dance studios, Europe's largest dance library and a performing arts health centre – or if you've got two left feet and are just here for the architecture, take a guided tour.

Nearest station: Deptford
Address: Creekside, SE8 3DZ
Architect: Herzog & de Meuron (2003)
Access: Free entry; paid guided tours,
pre-booking essential
Visitor info: trinitylaban.ac.uk

31

THE SHARD

A revolutionary glass-clad pyramid

Whether you think it's a masterpiece or an eyesore, it is impossible to ignore The Shard – a trailblazing fixture on the city's skyline. Renzo Piano's 95-storey glass tower was dreamed up by the Sellar Property Group (with a little help from the State of Qatar), and, like similar projects, has attracted heaps of speculation – the £50-million apartments are rumoured to remain unsold. It's also ushered a radical redevelopment of the London Bridge area, which has seen hip independent bars and restaurants move in. Stay in the hotel, indulge at one of six restaurants, or get vertigo from level 72's viewing platform.

Nearest station: London Bridge
Address: 32 London Bridge Street, SE1 9SG
Architect: Renzo Piano (2012)
Access: Restaurants and shops open to the public;
paid viewing gallery, pre-booking essential
Visitor info: the-shard.com

32

BATTERSEA POWER STATION

Cultural temple of power

Featured on Pink Floyd's *Animals* album cover, this Industrial landmark is the sum of two parts, erected in the 1920s and 1950s. In the 1980s, power station smoke ceased and it became the subject of much redevelopment debate, only recently realised. The drastic revamp is ongoing, and requires architectural masterminds: including Frank Gehry and Foster & Partners, among others, who both have projects in the riverside neighbourhood. Plans include a tube station, housing and a tower viewing platform. Keep track of progress from the train over Chelsea Bridge; or visit Circus West Village for a taste of what's to come.

Nearest station: Battersea Park
Address: 188 Kirtling Street, SW8 5BN
Architects: J. Theo Halliday and
Sir Giles Gilbert Scott (1955), various (ongoing)
Access: Restaurants and bars open to the public
Visitor info: batterseapowerstation.co.uk

33

THE NATIONAL THEATRE

A Brutalist concrete dream

If a Brutalist day out is your idea of a good time, then these labyrinthine concrete giants have it covered. The architecture also functions as infrastructure: The National Theatre connects to Southbank Centre and Waterloo Bridge via spiral staircases, passageways and terraces with vast riverside panoramas. It's a mighty celebration of public space. All routes lead to the biggest of the three theatres, the Olivier – a fan-shaped Greek-style auditorium with incredible acoustics and an atmosphere to match. And for the encore, head outside, where the iconic silhouette lights up in colour every night.

Nearest station: Waterloo
Address: Upper Ground, SE1 9PX
Architect: Sir Denys Lasdun (1976)
Access: Free entry; paid entry to shows,
pre-booking advised
Visitor info: nationaltheatre.org.uk

34

NEWPORT STREET GALLERY

Damien Hirst's immaculate Victorian revamp

The Stirling Prize-winning space makes a statement in the backstreets of Vauxhall. A clever conversion of three listed Victorian scenery-painting studios, which used to supply London's West End, the industrial terrace is topped with a saw-toothed roof, angled just-so to resemble toppling dominos. An LED screen lights up the exterior, while inside it's the full Damien Hirst package: climb to the top of a meticulous spiral staircase, explore his eclectic art collection for free across six galleries, and stop for a cocktail in the psychedelic Pharmacy 2 – complete with Hirst's signature 1990s Medicine Cabinets and kaleidoscope butterfly paintings.

Nearest station: Lambeth North
Address: Newport Street, SE11 6AJ
Architect: Caruso St John Architects (2015)
Access: Free entry
Visitor info: newportstreetgallery.com

35

THE CHAPEL

A divine Victorian reinvention

Rising architectural stars, Craftworks, have taken a disused, unconsecrated Victorian chapel in a quiet corner of south east London and transformed it into a modern home that still retains a sense of spirituality. A soaring, angular roof dominates the space, refracting natural light through the skylights with Gothic drama; while many of the religious relics – the pulpit, confessional, altar, organ and matroneum – have been resurrected in a domestic guise, allowing for synergy and functionality. Amen to that, we'd happily move in.

Nearest station: Denmark Hill
Address: Grove Park, SE5 8LH
Architects: John Belcher (1862), Craftworks (2018)
Access: Free entry during Open House
(check website as it may not be included every year)
Visitor info: openhouselondon.org.uk

36

SOUTH LONDON GALLERY

Fire station becomes sausage factory then gallery

Dating from 1867, this is the earliest, purpose-built fire station still standing in London. When sliding poles and hot water became a prerequisite, however, its fire-fighting days were over; and it became a sausage factory from 1934 to 2007. After falling derelict, it was donated to South London Gallery and subtly remodelled by 6a Architects in 2018. The expansion has made way for an archive gallery, artist's studio and community projects. Over the road, another 19th century dwelling is the original SLG building which offers up brunch and Mexican artist Gabriel Orozco's geometric garden.

Nearest station: Peckham Rye
Address: 65-67 Peckham Road, SE5 8UH
Architects: Godfrey Pinkerton (1891),
6a Architects (2010/2018)
Access: Free entry
Visitor info: southlondongallery.org

37

PECKHAM LIBRARY

A Futuristic neighbourhood escape

This spaceship-esqe structure landed in the urban sprawl of south east London in 2000, winning the Stirling Prize the same year and kicking off a fun future for 21st-century community architecture. It's now an established Peckham landmark, taking visitors on a journey to a new realm via its copper-clad L-shaped silhouette, with technicoloured glazing on one side and stilts on the other. Inside are three raised sycamore-veneer pods, housing cave-like reading rooms for storytelling, community meetings or just hiding away with your favourite architecture book (hello!).

Nearest station: Peckham Rye
Address: 122 Peckham Hill Street, SE15 5JR
Architect: Alsop & Störmer (2000)
Access: Free entry

38

GOLDSMITHS CENTRE FOR CONTEMPORARY ART

Victorian baths turned art gallery

This experimental art centre was created by Assemble, who transformed the cast-iron water tanks and service areas of the Victorian-era Laurie Grove Baths in 2017. Raw brickwork, corrugated pink cladding and teal pipes bring contemporary flair; and the diverse industrial spaces allow for a fresh exhibiting and viewing experience (it's free, too). Part of the Goldsmiths campus, expect to find art grads in the former bathing halls – still with original tiles – now used as the students' studio. And while you're here, have a look at the steel scribble-topped Ben Pimlott building next door.

Nearest station: New Cross Gate
Address: St James's, SE14 6AD
Architects: Thomas Dinwiddy (1898), Assemble (2018)
Access: Free entry
Visitor info: gold.ac.uk/goldsmithscca

39

SERPENTINE SACKLER GALLERY

Neoclassical rebirth with a twist

This lakeside art gallery is the perfect architectural juxtaposition, a synthesis of old – the Classical 19th-century brick gunpowder store, first built in 1805 – and new – a 21st-century glass-walled extension. Designed by the queen of curves, Zaha Hadid, the undulating glass-fibre woven textile roof is integral, setting a light, cohesive mood, while connecting gallery and event space to the café. Crowds head to Kensington Gardens for the annual summer pavilions by international architects, but the Serpentine Sackler and its leafy surrounds are definitely a year-round destination.

Nearest station: Lancaster Gate
Address: West Carriage Drive, W2 2AR
Architect: Zaha Hadid Architects (2013)
Access: Free entry
Visitor info: serpentinegalleries.org

40

ISMAILI CENTRE

Soothing Modernism in South Kensington

While the V&A, Natural History Museum and
Albert Memorial – all within walking distance –
often hog the limelight here, the small but mighty
Ismaili Centre goes about things a little more
discreetly. The architecture is a sublime marriage of
Western and Islamic aesthetics, and although deco-
ration is kept to a minimum (a requirement from
religious leader Aga Khan), there are subtle nods to
tradition such as the granite exterior, geometric
detailing at the entrance and the rooftop garden,
modelled around a central, serene fountain.

Nearest station: South Kensington
Address: 1-7 Cromwell Gardens, SW7 2SL
Architect: Hugh Casson and Neville Conder (1985)
Access: View from street (no public access)

41

DESIGN MUSEUM

A Modernist masterpiece reimagined

Set under the former Commonwealth Institute's hyperbolic paraboloid roof (technical term for 'sweeping curves'), the original interiors of this building have been stripped back to make way for a minimalist facelift. The redesign was controversial – with some backlash about the fast-and-loose approach to the conservation of Grade II listed features – but the result is wildly impressive. Find great contemporary design in the galleries, headspace in the triple-height atrium, and of course, coffee in the café, overlooking Holland Park.

Nearest station: High Street Kensington
Address: 224-238 Kensington High Street, w8 6AG
Architects: Robert Matthew and Stirrat Johnson-Marshall
& Partners (1962), John Pawson and OMA (2016)
Access: Free entry; paid entry to temporary exhibitions
Visitor info: designmuseum.org

42

WALMER YARD

Boutique residential block

Set in a discreet courtyard in Notting Hill, these four interlocking houses are a celebration of real craftsmanship. The project offers a fresh take on sequential space: exposed concrete walls were poured in situ, wooden-clad façades are interrupted by vertical shutters that play with light and shade. Exploring the structure is a multi-sensory experience. You can rent one (or all four) of the experimental lodges for an overnight stay and funds go directly to resident charity, The Baylight Foundation, which aims to increase public understanding of the power of architecture.

Nearest station: Latimer Road
Address: 235-239 Walmer Road, W11 4EY
Architects: Peter Salter and Fenella Collingridge (2016)
Access: Paid entry to events, pre-booking essential;
available for holiday lets
Visitor info: walmeryard.co.uk

43

MICHELIN HOUSE

A playful Art Deco palace

Brightening up the Fulham Road with its whimsical heritage, this building is larger than life in the best possible way. Home to the Michelin Tyre Company Ltd HQ until 1985, it was designed by employee, engineer François Espinasse, who allegedly had no architectural training before creating this early example of reinforced concrete construction. The exterior includes stained glass windows that riff on the retro adverts featuring Bibendum, aka Michelin Man, and cream tiles stamped with vintage racing cars. Inside, explore Conran's design emporium and stay for a fancy lunch at the restaurant, Bibendum.

Nearest station: South Kensington
Address: 81 Fulham Road, SW3 6RD
Architect: François Espinasse (1911)
Access: Restaurant and shop open to the public

44

WESTMINSTER UNDERGROUND STATION

Gotham City subway

Deep within this underground interchange that links the Circle, District and Júbilee lines is a world that sees the staircases of Hogwarts meet the futurism of Gotham City. Think smooth stainless steel escalators and columns, rough concrete walls and a web of diagonal beams and buttresses. Hopkins Architects call the whole effect 'Piranesian', inspired by the etchings of surreal labyrinthine prisons by 18th-century Italian artist Giovanni Battista Piranesi. The station has certainly upped the game for commuters, transporting them to street level where Westminster's mighty gothic counterparts, the Palace and Big Ben, pick up the baton and run with it.

Address: Westminster, SW1A 2JR
Architect: Hopkins Architects (1999)
Access: Open to the public (ticket required)

45

TRELLICK TOWER

The tower to define all Brutalist towers

Yes, it was once dubbed the 'tower of terror' due to crime, but Trellick wins you over in that rough diamond kind of way. Built with the future of city living in mind, Goldfinger took cues from Le Corbusier's 1950s Unité d'Habitation in France, creating 31 storeys of concrete that take into account sun, space and greenery. His most innovative move was placing the disruptive elements (lifts, bins and boilers) in a separate block. It's an urban icon that's had real social impact; while frequent pop culture references continue to boost its street cred.

Nearest station: Westbourne Park
Address: Golborne Road, W10 5PB
Architect: Ernö Goldfinger (1972)
Access: Free entry during Open House
(check website as it may not be included every year)
Visitor info: openhouselondon.org.uk

46

ROYAL INSTITUTE OF BRITISH ARCHITECTS (RIBA)

A serene Modernist retreat

This Fitzrovia HQ is pure style and sophistication. The pale Portland stone façade contrasts with the drama of the interior; opulent with marble, glass and brass Art Deco features and elegantly lit thanks to giant windows. Lose yourself in the extensive library, designed like an ocean liner (a precursor to the architect's later work on RMS Queen Elizabeth). Much more than a club for architecture aficionados, there's a wealth of exhibitions, talks and tours – and if nothing else, it's a welcome sanctuary from the chaos of nearby Oxford Street.

Nearest station: Regent's Park
Address: 66 Portland Place, W1B 1AD
Architects: George Grey Wornum and James Woodford (1934)
Access: Free entry; paid guided tours, pre-booking essential
Visitor info: architecture.com

47

HOOVER BUILDING

Art Deco off the A40

A dual-carriageway might not be the obvious place for an archi-tour, but lo and behold: the Hoover Building. Originally the vacuum cleaner's HQ in the 1930s, by the 1980s Tesco moved in and, conveniently, there's still a store at the back. Where else can you shop for groceries in an Art Deco monument? In 2015, part of the building was transformed into luxe apartments. The heritage features – grand staircases with wrought-iron banisters and terrazzo flooring – have polished up beautifully, and the green-and-black geometric details run from the neo-Egyptian façade throughout. Look out for its bright white cement ('snowcrete') finish next time you drive by.

Nearest station: Perivale
Address: Western Avenue, UB6 8AT
Architects: Wallis, Gilbert & Partners (1933),
Interrobang (2018)
Access: Restaurant and shops open to the public

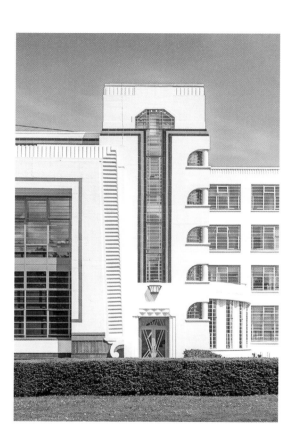

48

KEW GARDENS

Tropical World Heritage site

A powerful botanical lab, Kew Gardens is constantly growing. After a five-year restoration that would've made Queen Vic proud – repairing thousands of panes of glass, ironwork and paving – Temperate House, the world's largest Victorian glasshouse, reopened in 2018. The Palm House (restored in 1956 after bomb, humidity and insecticide damage) follows the same structure, with its own jungle climate. Elsewhere, the immersive Hive – a 17-metre-tall aluminium installation by artist Wolfgang Buttress – pays tribute to Britain's endangered honey bees. Set in a wildflower meadow, it is inset with 1,000 LED lights that glow to mimic the vibrations of the on-site hive.

Nearest station: Kew Gardens
Address: Royal Botanic Gardens, TW9 3AE
Architects: Decimus Burton (1860) amongst others
Access: Paid entry, pre-booking optional
Visitor info: kew.org

49

COAL DROPS YARD

1850s rail warehouse conversion

No doubt the coal-workers of the mid-1800s, 1930s factory girls and 1980s ravers, who all used this space over the years, would find it hard to recognise the vast Victorian industrial structures today. But Heatherwick Studio's transformation has left traces: from the outline of long-gone warehouse signs, to the cast-iron columns under old railway arches and the painted walls of Bagley's nightclub. Tiles touch mid-air, raising the roof for independent stores, pop-ups and restaurants. Expect to bump into the likes of Tom Dixon's HQ staff, residents of Gasholders apartments, Central Saint Martins students – and maybe a few ghosts.

Nearest station: King's Cross St Pancras
Address: Stable Street, N1C 4DQ
Architect: Heatherwick Studio (2018)
Access: Free entry
Visitor info: coaldropsyard.com

50

ROYAL COLLEGE
OF PHYSICIANS

The medics' Modernist/Brutalist triumph

On the corner of Regent's Park, Denys Lasdun's Royal College of Physicians bucks the Regency trend of the other parkside architecture in style. The floating horizontal blocks of concrete and glass atop a colonnaded portico are the subject of much debate: is it a Brutalist or Modernist structure? The million dollar question. We're in the Modernist camp; but for all its grand design, Lasdun was apparently more preoccupied with the building's functionality, inspired by the College's ceremonial and organisational needs. Explore medical motifs in the museum, and wander through the 1,000+ plants in the surrounding gardens.

Nearest station: Great Portland Street
Address: 11 St Andrews Place, NW1 4LE
Architect: Sir Denys Lasdun (1964)
Access: Free entry
Visitor info: rcplondon.ac.uk

51

BAPS SHRI SWAMINARAYAN MANDIR (NEASDEN TEMPLE)

A Hindu marble sanctuary

Fancy a trip to India? Driving up the North Circular to this Hindu temple is quicker than catching a flight, and almost as transportive. A phenomenal example of religious architecture, tradition lies at the heart of the temple's purist composition. Eight-thousand tonnes of Italian Carrara and Indian marble, Bulgarian limestone and Sardinian granite were first sent to India for artisans to carve its 26,300 pieces, before shipping over to the UK for construction between 1993 and 1995. They must have had some higher power on their side, alongside creator Pramukh Swami Maharaj, to pull off such an incredible feat of engineering.

Nearest station: Stonebridge Park
Address: 105-119 Brentfield Road, NW10 8LD
Architect: C. B. Sompura (1995)
Access: Free entry (modest dress essential)
Visitor info: londonmandir.baps.org

52

ISOKON FLATS

Hampstead's Modernist monument

Walking by this whitewashed, cruise ship-like structure, it is easy to see why the Modernist movement felt so radical at the time. Designed as an experiment in minimalist urban living, the reinforced concrete flats contrast with Belsize Park's Georgian terraces, yet still feel at ease with the area. In the 1940s, Lawn Road Flats (as it was then known) was home to artists, writers, architects and, rumour has it, spies seeking refuge from Nazi Germany. At the ground floor gallery, learn about the building's crafted form, and the free thinkers that lived inside including Bauhaus members Walter Gropius and Marcel Breuer, and author Agatha Christie.

Nearest station: Belsize Park
Address: Lawn Road, NW3 2XD
Architects: Wells Coates (1934), Avanti Architects (2004)
Access: Free entry to gallery
Visitor info: isokongallery.co.uk

53

HIGHGATE CEMETERY

A beautiful, faded celebration of the deceased

Burial grounds and architecture might not seem to go hand in hand, but this cemetery – one of London's 'Magnificent Seven' – hosts some exceptional funerary structures and headstones to die for. Pop artist Patrick Caulfield's quite literally reads 'DEAD' in playful typography, and Karl Marx lies here, too. There's the Grade I listed Egyptian Avenue, etched with exotic death motifs; and the Circle of Lebanon's opulent sunken tombs, built around an ancient tree. Book a tour of the west side for extra spooks and a BTS exploration of the eclectic occupants. And watch out for architect Nick Eldridge's contemporary glass house overlooking the ghouls.

Nearest station: Archway
Address: Swain's Lane, N6 6PJ
Architect: Stephen Geary (1839)
Access: Paid entry; for West Cemetery pre-book a tour
Visitor info: highgatecemetery.org

54

KENWOOD HOUSE

A Neoclassical retreat in a sublime park

Overlooking Hampstead Heath (one of London's oldest and greatest green spaces), this Neoclassical villa is a paean to community spirit. It's free to visit – a non-negotiable set by Edward Cecil Guinness (the late chairman of the brewery), who saved the house from demolition in 1925, making it a public gallery for his personal art collection. Echoes of the last family to live here, The Mansfields, can be felt in the creamy pink and blue ceilinged library, the red velvet-clad dining room and the off-site former dairy. It's also a beautiful vantage point to survey Humphry Repton's landscaped gardens, dating back to the 1790s.

Nearest station: Golders Green
Address: Hampstead Lane, NW3 7JR
Architects: John Bill (early 17th century),
Robert Adam (1779)
Access: Free entry
Visitor info: english-heritage.org.uk/kenwood

INDEX

(in alphabetical order)

An Opinionated Guide to London Architecture

First edition, second printing

First published in 2019 by Hoxton Mini Press, London
www.hoxtonminipress.com
Copyright © Hoxton Mini Press 2019. All rights reserved.
Text by Sujata Burman and Rosa Bertoli
Design and sequence by Daniele Roa
Text editing by Farah Shafiq and Faith McAllister
Production by Anna De Pascale
All photography © Taran Wilkhu except images below:

Aeriel view of the City of London, pp.4-5 © istock.com/_ultraforma_; Sir John
Soane's Museum © Gareth Gardner; Lloyd's of London (interior), no copyright;
Bloomberg HQ © James Newton/Bloomberg; 20 Fenchurch Street (interior)
© Holly Clarke and Sky Garden; Whitechapel Gallery © Guy Montagu-Pollock
at Arcaid, courtesy Whitechapel Gallery; Wilton's Music Hall (interior)
© Peter Dazeley; Tate Modern (exterior with river) © istock.com/godrick;
Eltham Palace © Historic England Photo Library (interior), © English Heritage
(exterior); Battersea Power Station © istock.com/_violinconcertono3;
The Chapel © Edmund Sumner; Design Museum (exterior) © Shruti
Veeramachineni Gravity Road; Westminster Underground Station © Getty
Images; Kew Gardens © David Post; Kenwood House © English Heritage

With thanks to Becca Jones for editorial and production support
and Matthew Young for initial series design

ISBN: 978-1-910566-55-8

Printed and bound by OZGraf, Poland